TOO MANY NEGATIVE PEOPLE

DARIELLE ARCHER

ISBN-13: 978-0-9978035-7-0

INTRODUCTION

We cannot always avoid negative people in our day-to-day activities. Even if your place of business or work environment is primarily positive, negative people will still exist to pull you down: clients, suppliers, neighbors or someone at the other end of the telephone. If not at work or home, then you are certain to come across negative statements or attitudes while standing in line at the store or attending parties, meetings, and other social gatherings. Most people have at least one relative who always seems to have a definite energy that can destroy even the happiest of moods with a single remark or gesture. The only way to combat this negativity is by recognizing when others are affecting your emotional balance and then protecting yourself by making psychic self-defense a natural habit.

As you learn to recognize the frequent presence of negativity and its inroads into your own wellbeing, you will seek to control them by taking the necessary steps. You will also find yourself able to scan your past and find instances of such things that you had never at the time imagined to be such.

The techniques you can use to defend yourself from too many negative people are easy to learn and simple to use. Best of all, they can be fun and uplifting.

THE BENEFITS OF PSYCHIC SELF-DEFENSE

Before getting underway, you might first want some clarification as to what psychic self-defense is, who needs it, and why.

Have you ever walked into a room and immediately known you didn't want to be there? Or have you visited someone's house and instantly felt uncomfortable? Or has there been a gift you inherited and the moment you touched it you were certain it could never be yours?

Basically, psychic self-defense is a way, an art, of protecting yourself from the sensed but unseen effects caused by the presence of negative people around you.

Everybody—living or deceased—has a certain amount of energy, and you can pick up that energy in many ways. Energy can be passed kinetically through objects. This is our most familiar exposure to it. It is not always passed through direct physical contact, but it can also be transmitted psychically. This explains why we can pick up that energy from a room or a gift or some other seemingly nonpersonal item. Without seeing or hearing an individual, we often can pick up on that person's energies.

Not all of these energies, by any means, are good. In fact, a great deal of them are negative. Techniques of psychic self-defense can be used to help you cope with the everyday needs and demands for protection that we all have. Although you cannot see the effects of these negative people, you definitely can feel them.

At various times we find ourselves capable of a greater or lesser amount of self-protection. You are more vulnerable to negativity if you are depressed, tired, or recovering from an illness. At such times you are more prone to feel the effects of negative people in your sphere of activity. It is important that you know how to guard yourself.

What you will learn is how to strengthen yourself. It is similar to building good health. Psychic self-defense can help your business life, home life, and love life. In fact, it can become a tool for enhancing the learning and growth in all the basic areas of your life. By helping you distinguish energy and emotions more easily, the art of psychic self-defense offers you more control over your life. Its techniques are basic tools toward promoting a much richer, happier life.

PEOPLE PRONE TO COLLECTING NEGATIVITY

Without self-protection, vulnerable people can accumulate more and more negative energy, somewhat like a carpet that stores static electricity in cold weather.

Out of modern society's wide spectrum, some groups of people are more prone to suffering from the effects of negative people than others. Mothers, for instance, and more specifically, housewives, might be ranked in this class. Their energies are in great demand from husband, children, and home. A mother doesn't usually concern herself with her own protection, and this makes her an open field. She may think she is upset or experiencing frustration when often what she is really feeling are the effects of other people's energies in her house.

Very creative people are prone to collecting negativity. Because true creativity and sensitivity are so closely linked, many artists run a double risk: not only are they sensitive (almost by definition) but also they are less shielded. Often while they are absorbed in their creative efforts, they fail to take note of their immediate surroundings. Unguarded in the face of repeated negative assaults, they have accumulated a great deal of negative energy. By the time the distracted artists come around to feeling this energy, it is more intense, for they feel it with the full power of their native sensitivity.

Techniques of psychic self-defense might also be useful to people who work in sales. All types of sales—including real estate, marketing and retail sales—have a great amount of negative energy as an occupational hazard. The skilled salesperson is able to counter all of this. When you met or hear of people in this profession who have great energy, never tire, and step from one goal to the next, you are encountering people who have instinctively trained themselves. Out of necessity, and with a degree of innate aptitude, they have developed the ability to unconsciously protect themselves. Aware of it or not, they practice many techniques of psychic self-defense.

People who protect themselves on a daily basis are rarely robbed or victimized. You can counteract the possibility of becoming a victim with some of the techniques that follow.

IDENTIFYING NEGATIVE FIELDS

At this point it is important not to rush. (If I'd wanted you to rush this would be a long book, a flood of facts, challenging you to run rapidly from one end to the other. But that's not the aim. Here, the focus is simplicity. The essence is here; the extension will be all yours.)

Now, don't rush. Don't tear your room apart in search of pen or pencil. But do find, in a leisurely way, a writing stick you're comfortable with and a scratch pad or something along those lines.

Relax now, and get comfortable.

In this relaxed posture, begin writing down those areas of your life in which you feel out of control, where you suspect that an unfortunate pattern might be repeating itself, where you feel as though you are a victim or a victim-in-waiting.

Do you have a boss, for instance, who overpowers you the moment you walk into work? Do you feel yourself cringing and withdrawing, an actual reaction in the region of the stomach or the neck? Do you have encounters with someone you like but find yourself exhausted every time you walk away? Or is there some house you visit where the people are amiable, but the visit still leaves you upset? Or is there a place you pass as you drive down the road where you get a sudden and strong feeling that something is not right?

Identifying the common situations where you are not feeling in complete control of your emotions is the start of being able to recognize all areas where negativity has its effects on you. Recognition is important in establishing your defense.

Continue to relax. Deep breathing here plays an important role. Take deep, full breaths. See yourself standing by a doorway breathing in fresh air. As you breathe deeply you are instilling the vital life force. The charge of air to the lungs is your ability to symbolically take in life. As you breathe deeply, in this conscious effort, it is a slowing down, a stilling of the self. Take each thought, one by one, and begin to work on it. Whatever you are feeling at this time of breathing, write it down.

What about your thoughts on developing psychic defenses? Does this feel like something you want to learn? Does it scare you? Write down what is coming to your mind.

Take note how the room feels. What does it feel like to be with yourself? Earlier today, what did it feel like when standing or seated next to another person?

Catalogue your own responses. Recognition of these responses gives you a sense of your boundaries, and boundaries are critical in establishing your defenses.

SIMPLE TECHNIQUES

A. *Cloaking Technique*

One of the first techniques you can use is the "cloak." One of my favorites is The Great Old Cloak From England. This is truly a cloak without daggers. It is wonderful to see. To see it you must create it yourself. (Remember, in the physics of Aristotle and other ancients, sight didn't proceed from objects to the passive eye, but actively outward from the eye to the object.)

You want to visually build a cloak of colors that surrounds your body and instills a sense of safety, security, and protection. For myself, I picture the cloak as on a wasteland moor, the cloak all colorful, winds whipping all around—the winds of negative energy. The aural cloak can be built anywhere.

One of the colors you will want to use to build your aural field is white. White is for purity. Yet it is purity founded on the presence of all colors. White is a reflective color. Blue is equally important. Blue is a communication color, associated with our throat chakra. Blue enhances our abilities to see and then to say to others what we are experiencing. Knowing that communication through the cloak is desirable should tell you something about the fabric of which the cloak is made. London Fog doesn't sell one. But you can make your own—one that provides you with shelter and security yet does not isolate you from others.

B.   *Zip-Lock Bag*

A variant cloak, less flamboyant, but equally effective, is the zip-lock bag. It is especially good for situations of interpersonal stress. Step into your zip-lock bag, bring your hand across the top, carrying the zipper, and you're sealed. A jingle here might come to mind: you can boil, bake, or freeze them, but you can't hurt the goods inside. (Notice, you are not sealing yourself into a dark green Hefty Sack.)

This transparent, thin bag allows you to listen and comprehend the feelings of those outside. This is not an escapist trick to refuse all dealings with reality, but neither do anger, antipathies, and fears of others have to flood all over you, triggering your own fears, angers, and antipathies. The zip-lock bag allows you to deal with the miserable without becoming the kind of company they are rightly said to love. The zip-lock bag allows you to stay fresh even in the presence of the hottest or sulkiest air. Suppose someone is telling you the same story you've heard for the last year or two, "I'm so miserable, life is awful . . . ," yet the person has done nothing to change any of this. Inside the sheathing of your bag you can for a moment think of a happy or funny incident in your life and in seconds be back for the continuation of the saga. Here, you can listen and achieve an even clearer understanding because you have allowed a distance for perspective. Here, you don't have to breathe the air of the lowlands, and you are free to judge or think without insidious interference or meddling.

Cloaks are cerebral garments, yet must grow from the individual heart. They must soothe and protect, but not veil. Just so, you might walk the sands to the pyramids, a parasol in one hand.

C.   *Necessary Clothes and Symbolism*

So far, you have seen suggestions for projected defenses of a symbolic nature. Yet we have access, mandatory in our society, to less heady defenses, and these are clothes. You've heard a lot about Power Suits and Power Dressing. And the fact is there's a lot of truth to it, so much that we're damn near over-Powered. Myself, I don't advocate Power Dressing, with its capital P and D. I don't want to run around overpowering people. I hope you don't either. For with so many people powering around, we're likely only to end up with a society little different from that of the mindless balls on a billiard table.

My suggestion, and my practice, is to dress with a ratification of self. This gives something to other people and at the same time prevents you from being steamrolled by others. When you get dressed, you want to claim everything you touch so that it has your vibration. Whatever you wear you say, "I am claiming this. Yes, this is mine. This is me. This day I wear this vibration." People will respect this even unconsciously.

This is why you can discover a great deal about people because of their colors, even if they are wearing suits. Several people might have the same shade on, but one, having claimed that suit, will wear it lighter and brighter and wear it with a different attitude than the others who have not claimed it.

Remember, there is a huge difference between a coat hanger and a human being. A coat hanger does not change the garments put onto it. A human being, through choice, through claiming and rejecting, touches and changes everything in its radius.

D.   *Colors*

Colors are not restricted to objects or clothes. Yet clothes without colors do not exist. Select each color. Close your eyes. Focus on one color at a time: a whole field of each color. Again, don't rush. What do you see? What do you feel?

While colors might be described by Newtonian physics on an objective scale, no human being has ever seen a single color other than subjectively.

Astronomers deduce many things about far-away stars by analyzing light wavelengths. We should show equal or more smarts by noting our reactions to color. For, like it or not, we do react to color. The emotional and psychic effects of color are profound. In a sense, we are creatures of color. Why else would we see red when upset? And it's not just you. Everyone reacts. That's why it's so important to take care in selecting the colors we put out there.

Peach and pink are light, warm colors, symbolic of divine love and self-love. I suggest using lighter pinks, lilacs, golds, but always of iridescent and shimmering tones.

Orange is used to heal human relationships and your own relationship to your body at all times. This is really what you are trying to do, strengthen the physical and aural body.

Then surround yourself with a layer of white.

Next, add a layer of blue to communicate effectively what you are saying to all people. Blue is your expression color.

I like shimmering, iridescent colors that reflect back to the people you are around. "Sunlight on water" colors. Shimmer colors.

This is merely an outline of one possible color-recipe. It is one I use often. Yet, if you focus on colors, create colors, and use colors, you will be on the path to learning for yourself far more than any manual might set you upon. At the back you will find further hints on color and on their uses and effects.

E.   *Deep Breathing*

Everyone has to breathe. So why breathe like someone with respiratory problems, in brittle spare puffs? Though we all breathe for the duration of our lives most of us do it as if we ourselves had nothing to do with it at all. Breathe deeply. Pay attention to the inhalation, the exhalation, to even notice in this world, some connection to this universe.

As you deep breathe, on the inhale flex your toes toward your knee, and on the exhale point your toes down. This allows for the easy passage of energy from head to toe and reverse. This is a very calming and strengthening exercise. Do this breathing exercise for a minimum of five minutes.

Begin to use breathing even before you get out of bed. Ten or fifteen deep breaths are good. Begin to feel that strengthening, that invigoration, as it comes to you. See yourself from head to foot as surrounded by a glow, a glow you draw elastically in and out with each breath, this shimmering life force. Breathe it down over your heart, out into the body, and through the pores. Let your breathing give you a sense of control before you even leave your bed. Establish your breath, your pulse, as true and constant with this golden life force around you, and you will not find the daily course of chutes and ladders giving you anywhere near the usual amount of vertigo and stress.

F.   *Sea Salt*

There are processes using sea salt that can help you gain psychic protection. Especially when working with large groups of people, sea salt or borax can be used to help cleanse your aural field. If you have been in a very intense session, bringing you to feel literally "sticky" —a hard day in school, selling, being out in traffic, things aimed at you, the glares of strangers— you need to take actions to protect yourself through cleansing.

In the shower or bath, using either sea salt or borax, take a healthy handful and rub your neck and chest area and along your arms, and you will immediately feel lighter. I can't necessarily explain how this works, but it does work. Try it, you'll see. Also, at a party, or any gathering of people, you can set sea salt in small bowls and this will serve to keep the area clean. After the gathering be sure to throw away the salt.

Sea salt is also useful in changing the energy of a new house or a new office. It dispels negative energy that may have been left behind by the former occupants. You can bring love and health into your new house or office by literally going around the house with a teaspoon and sprinkling the floor with salt. Claim the place as yours and make a statement to affirm that the rooms are filled with love and positive benefits.

G.   *Symbolism In Psychic Self-Defense*

By now you may have noticed that this approach to self-defense is many layered. You have entered cloaks and zip-lock bags. You have absorbed and created colors, you have breathed deeply, and yet you have also considered such seemingly mundane things as sea salt and clothes.

Now can all these things be reconciled to an attack termed psychic? The defenses are many layered, because human beings are exactly that.

Psychic phenomena are not exclusively bound to operate on one plane or another but can enter our lives at all levels. Aspects of our lives are proportionately spiritual, mental, and physical. No facet is totally lacking in any of these three qualities. Sea salt applied to sullied skin is more physical, but not entirely so. Cloaks are proportionately more mental, but not entirely so. Colors are equally both, and more.

You are standing somewhere. You feel something bore right between your shoulders. You turn around and someone is in fact staring at you. How did you sense that? Of what qualities—spiritual, mental, physical—did that experience partake?

I'm not a hair-splitter, because I've seen too many people with incredible frizzies as a result. I'll give you what I've got, and you can draw your own conclusions, but the experiences are undeniable.

Now, some people suggest that rituals might be useful in combating psychic attacks. That may be so, but I prefer to use the mind. Rituals are effective later, at a time when you can use them, but projection can have just as great benefits. In modern society, rituals are untimely because encounters simply come too fast. It is just not feasible to perform rituals when we are in public places such as offices or grocery stores.

My own preference and emphasis is for creative personal symbolism. Not just any symbol, of course, will do. Symbols have lives of their own; we water them, grow them, stand protected in their shade, or climb to their tops for views.

In the sense that we create color, we can also create ourselves. We can nurture cloaks and bags—or by now you may have brought to your own mind some very suited vehicle for self-protection, a golden chariot or a sturdy elephant—all these things are there for our choosing, like good breathing, and they will very often meet us halfway. The mind is unlimited. If you have personal symbols that you want to use—stars or crosses or crescents—these work well. Use anything for which you have an affinity. Feel free to use any symbol you associate with protection. It is, after all, very personal to you.

Psychic self-defense involves some modes of outward behavior, but it more nearly concerns training of the mind. It comes from using techniques over and over until they become second nature.

When you begin to work with these you can learn to protect everything—your work, your home, your children, your car, even the people you associate with.

RECOGNIZING A PSYCHIC ATTACK

A lot of people ask, "How do you know if you are under a psychic attack?" A psychic attack should be suspected when things feel out of sequence for you. Sudden discomfort is a good clue. Often it will seem that nothing should be wrong, you may be having a good time yet you feel a disturbance whose source you cannot identify.

Generally, you will feel it in the area of the solar plexus. This is where our personal power is housed. Another place where you may feel the center of an attack is in the third eye. The assault will cause you to get a raging headache. Negative people don't want us to see the truth, and so we feel their energy in the area of the third eye or at the back of the head. For a mythic precedent, recall the story of Ulysses and the Cyclops.

Another place you may experience discomfort is the throat chakra. This results from an attack on your ability to express yourself. You may feel like you want to say something but you can't get it out. You may try to speak but only be able to stammer over your words.

Sometimes at a party there will be one person present who has an overwhelming amount of anger and bitterness. That person can infect the entire room or the whole house. You can counter this with the cloak, or more socially, with the zip-lock technique.

Some attacks are directed. People might send them because they are jealous of the way you look, of your occupation, or of your husband or children. We need to minimize the day-in and day-out effects of these envious aspects. And remember, these people not only saturate themselves but also their desks, their things, and the places where they sit. Confronted by such a person, or one of their proxy objects, it is best to stop and take fifteen deep breaths. This will brace you and change your energy. This is the equivalent of a psychic calisthenic. You are building psychic health.

Some attacks, which will still be felt as attacks, are not specifically directed. Oftentimes people are not setting out to attack with malice, but their thoughts, spilling over onto others, have the same effect. Even under a positive veneer, a great many people continue to exude the negative whininess of a character such as Hardy Har Har. Remember Hardy Har Har? The hyena? He was Lippy the Lion's cohort. He walked with a forward stoop, a kind of lumbering step. His eyes bent to the ground, always putting the worst construction on everything. "Oh, me," he always said, "Oh my, oh Lippy, we're do oooooo med." Even if people aren't saying this, they are often thinking this, and thoughts are real. Just because we can't see them doesn't mean they aren't there. And in a way, these nonspecific attacks are more difficult to combat. You might not be able to find verbal or visual confirmation of the person's negativity, and your inclination might be to disregard what you are feeling. Don't.

A lot of what we perceive as psychic attacks are not really attacks. We have simply moved too close to a person who has a great deal of negativity. Some people go around with every channel open and let everything enter. This would be great if you were in a world full of nothing but sainted angels, but you're not. You must learn to filter. Acknowledge the negative, but don't invite it home. If you send it packing before it moves in, life is a whole lot easier.

ESTABLISHING BOUNDARIES

By setting some boundaries you can keep from absorbing the negativity of those you come into contact with each day. Even physical boundaries are important. Take some string, not actual string, mind you, but mental string: bright, tight, well-defined, and colorful. Setting yourself at the center, establish your perimeters of physical space. At what point is someone too close?

Here is one of those instances where physical and emotional issues are hopelessly intertwined. Why is it some people you know can cross the strings to touch you, but when certain others do it you want to push them halfway back across the world? Yet here is your intruder, inside your strings. You step back. The intruder follows. Evidently the intruder doesn't notice or doesn't care. At this point you may want to put out your hand and say, "Back, please." But that might be considered rude, and a display of great weakness on your part for not having kept him out of your space in the first place.

This is a good example of a need for the zip-lock bag. You don't need your strings. They just set a general rule. When that rule has been violated, you know you need stronger medicine. Put on your zip-lock bag and seal yourself, or put on your cloak and shine brightly. Shine so he can't stand it. Soon the intruder will himself feel intruded upon, and he will back away. Without a word you will have vanquished an assault, without having made an enemy, without physical or even verbal violence. You will have the added satisfaction of watching someone who is probably used to manipulating others scratch his head, having backed off, but not quite sure why.

For boundaries we can also use another technique that I call "sitting under a rainbow." This is best when at a desk or work place. I often have a five-foot rainbow on the corners of my desk and see myself sitting under that rainbow. When people call me on the phone with their problems, I am able to maintain the rainbow's radiance myself and help pass it on to others. I remain healthy under it, and others benefit from its light.

In an environment you detect as hostile you can put up boundaries of reflective black glass or mirrors: you can look out just fine, but those around you will encounter two phenomena: (1) the color will absorb their energies before reaching you, and (2) what remains of their energies will be reflected back at them. Mentally defend yourself this way and you will avoid participation in overt antagonism. If anything, the person looking for a fight will have to fight himself as reflected from the black glass.

GROUPS

There are also such things as group boundaries. A church might be considered the prime example of the function of group boundaries. A church is a group of people bound together by ideas, by practices, even by buildings tailored to the common needs of the group.

Any group has its common ideas, aims, and commitments. Yet not all groups have special buildings established for their functions. Short of this, it is a good idea to always begin any meeting by verbalizing the priorities, the purposes, of a group. The people who have come have taken the trouble to be there, and so a moment of silence in the recognition of that effort is a good way to help affirm the group's identity.

Before I go to meetings I think are important, I try to arrive early enough to "clean out" any negative energy that might be present beforehand. What I generally do is visualize the room as bathed in a lavender or white flame. This is a purifying flame, not a randomly destructive one. At the same time I try to affirm the value of the meeting that is scheduled.

A group has an identity, just as a person has, only it is more vulnerable to centripetal forces. It is much easier for members of a group to walk away from each other than it is for a person to abandon himself. If there are those within a group trying to cause dissension it is important to let them try it openly. Don't deny the opportunity; don't get caught up in what they're sending. As a group, you might even wish to thank them. If the group is sound, a challenge is either reasonable and will lead to moderate reform, or it is needless and will be dismissed. If the group is unsound perhaps it's time for two groups, and two sets of boundaries. After all, do you want cats and dogs in the same carrier box?

As an individual in a group meeting you may find yourself receiving negative thoughts from someone else. You may feel as though someone is staring at you. If you feel uncomfortable, say you're feeling something from behind you, place yourself in a two-way mirrored cylinder. An attacker can look in but cannot get at you. This is going to feel alien to you for a time, but when you begin using such techniques on a regular basis, they will feel both effective and natural.

USING PSYCHIC DEFENSES AT WORK

Work is possibly the most important place where we need to make use of psychic defense techniques. Such techniques can forestall wrangling among equals and can also help to balance necessarily unequal boss/employee relationships.

It is the nature of a job to have people asking you to do things for them, although many times it's the wrong person asking you to do their work. How dare they? They dare because you are putting something out there that leads them to believe they can get away with it. You must establish your presence.

In situations of this sort find an image of strength and resilience. Myself, I choose the elephant. The elephant is sturdy, strong-limbed. The elephant is also intelligent. When some mongoose comes up to you (and you can usually see him coming, can't you?) brace yourself with a deep pachydermial breath. Look the mongoose in the eye. The mongoose is a little hyperactive thing. Hold your ground. Be prepared to utter the one syllable, if the request is out of line. Look at the mongoose. Watch him squirm, wiggling to find a way to make his request when he sees how unwelcome it is. Silence is your best ally, until you say "yes" or "no."

A good boss is like the elephant: firm, thoughtful, orderly. A good employee is also like the elephant. A team of elephants could move any stone in the world.

Unfortunately, there are too many mongooses running around, interfering. Often, we find these mongooses in the wrong places. These mongooses seem to think that just because they once killed a cobra they are fit to run the entire known universe.

Put the mongoose in his place. Look right through him. He will begin to sense his own emptiness. He will blush and skulk away. But he is habitual and will be back tomorrow, as full of noise and bluff as ever.

Every day you must level him with a steady eye. Soon, he will start barking up a different tree. You will have defeated him by letting him see himself, and he will not be able to say a word in complaint.

Cloaks and rainbows are fine techniques for the long hours spent in the workplace, but there are those inevitable moments when we must reach to the level of the animal world because the workplace is hierarchical by nature and demands it.

You should seek your own nature-image, your own totem. Look for it, and it will come to meet you halfway. You will know you have found the right one when you find both your strength and your compassion growing. Because you are stronger, you will find less to fear from feelings of compassion. Choose your character and build it. Together, you will hew a niche. And remember how important this is. Heraclitus, the Ionian philosopher, said it best: Character is Fate.

Sole Proprietorship

Say you have your own business. Say it. Is this true? Do you? Is it yours? Are you proud to be responsible for it? Look at what your business sends out. Are the services valuable? Are they performed in a way that helps other people? Or are the detrimental?

A business is an extension of self. Are you only in it for the money? Or are your various personal motives aligned in a more harmonious way? Establish the value of your business, and not solely from a monetary standpoint. Establish your aims and the needs to be fulfilled. Then, using psychic self-defense techniques, protect your business and develop it. It is worth protecting and deserves to grow.

Every morning come in and bless your business. Your customers and clients, consciously or not, will benefit from this. Use color. Place a rainbow over your business. This can be very effective. Never lose sight of the fact that you are a human being conducting transactions, not with inert objects, but with other human beings. From beneath a rainbow, it is hard to suffer from the tunnel vision so common to people running their own businesses. Under the rainbow sits a human being. At its two ends, where they belong, lie the pots of gold.

Diminishing Your Own Negative Thoughts

What if you are the one who is putting out energy that is less than positive? Most often when we do this it is because we feel threatened by another person or a particular situation. When you feel these negative inner trends, you want to examine the circumstances that caused them. Self-understanding is the first key to finding a way to cancel these thoughts, to diminish them. Ask yourself: why am I sending these thoughts? And just as importantly: am I hurting myself?

At times in our lives we are more susceptible to negative thoughts than at other times. Such trends have an unfortunate snowballing effect. It is important to counteract them before the trends become overwhelming, and a permanent way of life.

Often these negative thoughts come out as

criticism of those around us. If you find yourself deriding a person, out loud or not, look at that person and say, "You are a lesson to me, a mirror of something I dislike in myself." Perhaps you can't do much for the offending person, but you can alter your own attitudes, and that will eventually help you feel better about yourself.

You can help the process by surrounding a person who irritates you in a soft peach light. This is a healing color. To counter your own negative attitudes, bathe yourself in yellow. Yellow is like sunshine, a feeling of cheerfulness.

Everybody picks up the invisible thought-forms. It is important that you, too, are looking at what you are putting out, and then take responsibility for those thoughts.

Daily Use and Discipline

You—we together—have now done an exploratory on psychic self-defense as a way of combating the negative auras of other people. We have even seen how to nip our own negativity in its natal black bud.

Breathing, visualization, respect, and an acceptance of the strength of the reality of things we can't see all play a part in this discipline. This exploration has been something like digging a garden. We have dug in the soil together, and the seeds are planted. Yet it will require some further attentiveness on our part to come to a proper harvest.

We must each select what is valuable and develop the imagery proper to us. This will not be done overnight. It is a discipline that requires day-to-day applications. The remainder of this guide is composed of suggestions of such applications, with hints of color/powers an image/shields.

I hope to see your many rainbows soon.

SUGGESTIONS AND HINTS
FOR USING COLOR

Color is a great transformer of emotions. Make them shimmer like the sun's rays on water. All colors vibrate to different frequencies. People respond emotionally to colors you are physically wearing or even mentally thinking about. I generally use several colors, and in between each one I layer with white.

If you are trying to make friends or bring peace between yourself and a neighbor or colleague at work, a great way to do this is by sending out cheerful or loving colors.

With your children, especially with your teenagers, realize they are not attacking you; they are merely going through a learning time and need to test. See your child's room as a happy and cheerful place. In a room you want to purify, paint the walls white.

When you are feeling tired or sick or are recovering from an illness, spin a turquoise cocoon around yourself.

Use colors to communicate to others. Surround the person front and back. See pink around their heart. Rose is a good color to show unconditional love. Green is a heart regeneration color. Use turquoise for healing. Use blue to open the communication channels.

Use flowers to change the energy of a room. Bright cheery colors, like yellow, or dynamic colors, like red, can bring in warmth and life energy.

Color Glossary

White has all colors and is a reflector, a mirror. I use white a great deal since people often send negativity with no idea they are doing so. White is a good all-around cleanser: it works like an antiseptic. It represents cleanliness, newness, and purity.

Black absorbs all colors. Use black to absorb negativity. Black holds our power, keeping our images to ourselves. Wear black when you have a need to retain your strength or in times when you need more discipline and willpower.

Black and White – a perfect balance. Use them together when a person is feeling so down they seem lost. For these people I always use a black wall. It absorbs negativity. On the inside wall or the wall one faces toward, I often use pink for love, self love. Or sometimes I use peach as it has both pink, representing the home and nurturing, and orange, which heals and nourishes the physical body and relationships.

Gold – a high, strong energy. Determined, high value on life, success, noble, generous.

Silver – gentle, receptive, truth, candlelight, and dinner.

Gray or Tan – when you don't want people to know what you feel or you don't care to talk.

Brown – sensitive, honest, earthly. A liking for nature

and an enjoyment of the earth like the roots of a tree. Brown is a rich, grounding color, a color of structure, organization, and time management.

Maroon – use sparingly, a sensitive color that intensifies negative emotions. The overly sensitive should not wear maroon or wine.

Red – use it if you feel low on energy. It's bone marrow color. Red and black together are revitalizing. This energetic color makes your cells vibrate. It is an ambitious, excitable, courageous color. It is a dynamic color. Most people like red.

Mauve – people helpers. Encourages people to highest potential, gentleness.

Pink – loving, vulnerable, friendly, nurturing, and compassionate. Pink can be a very sensual color. It is nonthreatening, touchable.

Orange – an action color. Represents life organization and is used for healing. Helps to heal human relationships and your relationship to your body. Orange is talkative and social and shows consideration for others. An intense color for times requiring this strength and intensity.

Apricot or Peach – beach time, physical warmth, touching, talking. It shows you are approachable. Also helps one like one's own body. Peach shirts and towels are a great way to get in touch with your feelings around your body. Peach is generous, loving, sensual, and healing. Helps the body vibrate.

Yellow – personal power, sunshine, cheerful, warm, happy. Demonstrates a want to expand, share feelings. It's also a color of imagination and mental cheerfulness.

Green – regenerating and calming color. Think of a refreshing forest or fields of green. Green represents service to others; science, humanitarian, environmental issues.

Apple Green – (color of Granny Smith apples) outgoing, fun, and adaptable.

Pale Green – artistic and selfless. Pale green is a color of kindness and creativity.

Teal (more green than blue) – a color for times when a person feels sentimental but may not want to show it.

Turquoise (more blue than green) – this is the master healer. Represents cheerfulness and adventure. Turquoise is a dynamic, moving color.

Dark Blue – independent, self-sustaining. It is the color of the boss or the executive: commanding, motivating.

Light, Sky Blue – always creating or thinking, dreamer, great imagination, very analytical, artistic. This is a communication color, for analyzing and talking.

Purple – very intuitive or want to be more so, bringing up feelings. Takes away emotional/physical pain. Use sparingly.

The Thriving Code
A Guide for Healing and Energy Protection

"The Thriving Code" gives you a step-by-step powerful roadmap filled with techniques:

- *Learn the positive ways to defuse negative situations in everyday life.*
- *Discover ways to defend and protect yourself and those you love.*
- *Release yourself from the harmful effects of negative bosses, groups and energy vampires.*
- *The Codes show you how to use the energy in food, color, and days of the week.*
- *Discover how to use affirmations, visualization, self-hypnosis, and Feng Shui for protection.*
- *Develop a powerful mindset and learn about Chakras, Feng Shui, and gemstones for protection.*
- *Learn how to be prepared, feel safe, and relaxed.*

Using these amazing strategies will put the reader in the driver's seat.

Release and break free from harmful negativity.

Why wait to start living your life?

The Thriving Code

Available in paperback (978-09978035-3-2)
and for download (978-0-9978035-6-3)

About Darielle Archer
(Dariel Roskie)
CH, CNLP, CHC

Darielle is an author, motivational speaker,
breakthrough coach, and life strategist.
She is certified in hypnosis, NLP,
and Hypno-Coaching,
using the power of the conscious and
unconscious mind to achieve your dreams.

Author and Founder of

The Positive Works

SIGN UP FOR FREE
Stop Negativity Now Exercise

Please Visit For More Information:

Facebook: https://www.facebook.com/darielle1
Twitter: https://twitter.com/dariellearcher
The Positive Works Website: https://thepositive-
works.com/
https://thepositiveworks.com/blog/
and Good Changes Now Blog,
thepositiveworks.com

www.ingramcontent.com/pod-product-compliance
Lightning Source LLC
Chambersburg PA
CBHW051013050726
47592CB00007B/2836